ESSENTIAL 101 TIPS

HOME
DECORATING

ESSENTIAL 101 TIPS

HOME DECORATING

Nicholas Barnard

A DORLING KINDERSLEY BOOK

Editor Susie Behar
Art Editor Colin Walton
Series Editor Charlotte Davies
Managing Art Editor Amanda Lunn
Production Controller Louise Daly
US Editor Laaren Brown

First published in Canada in 1996 by
Fenn Publishing Company Ltd.
1090 Lorimar Drive, Mississauga, Ontario, Canada, L5S 1R8

ISBN 1-55168-046-7

Computer page makeup by Colin Walton Graphic Design, Great Britain
Text film output by Cooling Brown, Great Britain
Reproduced by Colourscan, Singapore
Printed and bound by Graphicom, Italy

ESSENTIAL TIPS

PREPARING TO PAINT

1 WHY PAINT?

Using paint is an easy, very economical, and effective way to decorate a room. There are many different types and colors of paint now available and a range of easy-to-do paint effects. Wall color can determine the character of a room: a light paint will give a small room a sense of spaciousness, while a dark color will make a large room seem cozier. Paint can also disguise flaws in walls and ceilings.

PAINT IS QUICK & EASY TO USE

2 HOW MUCH PAINT?

To estimate the amount that you will need, read the instructions, taking into account the number of coats required and the type of surface – a porous surface, for example, will need more paint than a surface that is nonporous. Useful guidelines are:
- Divide the room into units of the same color or type of paint.
- Multiply together the height and width of each unit.
- Add together the unit totals.

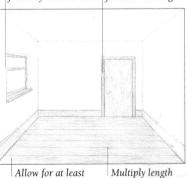

Calculate paint for frame by window area *Add an extra third for door moldings*

Allow for at least two coats of varnish on floor *Multiply length and width of floor for ceiling area*

3 PAINTING EQUIPMENT

It is worth investing in good quality equipment, especially brushes and rollers. If it costs too much, borrow or rent equipment.

½ IN (12 MM)   2 IN (50 MM)

ARTIST'S BRUSHES   VARNISHING BRUSH

 RADIATOR BRUSH

SANDPAPER

SPONGE

CORK BLOCK   SCRAPER & FILLING KNIFE   TSP

△ **PAINT & VARNISH BRUSHES**
Brush sizes range from 6 in (150 mm) to small artist's brushes required for details.

△ **SURFACE PREPARATION EQUIPMENT**
Proper surface preparation is important and will save you from redoing work later on.

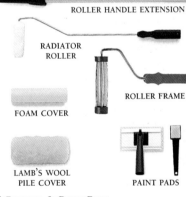

ROLLER HANDLE EXTENSION

RADIATOR ROLLER

ROLLER FRAME

FOAM COVER

LAMB'S WOOL PILE COVER   PAINT PADS

METAL TRAY

GLASS JAR   METAL PAINT BUCKET

△ **ROLLER TRAYS & CONTAINERS**
Decant paint into a paint bucket – you can decant just as much as you need.

△ **ROLLERS & PAINT PADS**
For large areas, you may prefer to use a roller or paint pad instead of a brush.

OTHER TOOLS ▷
Use a lint-free cloth to wipe surfaces, turpentine to clean off oil-based paint, doweling and muslin to prepare paint, and a flat-bladed knife to open the can.

LINT-FREE CLOTH

WOODEN DOWELING

FLAT-BLADED KNIFE

MASKING TAPE

TURPENTINE   COTTON MUSLIN

4 CONSIDER THE SURFACE TYPE

Different surfaces require different treatments. Bare wood should be sanded and then primed, while stained wood should be treated with wood bleach. Surface texture should match the character of a room; for example, smooth paintwork may not suit an old house.

BARE PLASTER
Brush, prime, and seal with diluted latex paint.

BARE BRICK
Brush to remove debris, and then coat with masonry paint.

TEMPERA
Scrape. Seal with stabilizing solution. Paint with latex.

WALLPAPER
Although stripping is best, nonvinyl can be painted over.

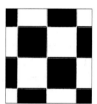

CERAMIC TILES
Coat with gloss or enamel, or strip for best results.

STAIN
Remove stain with wood bleach, seal, sand, and prime.

5 PREPARING A GOOD SURFACE

A painted surface that is in a good condition usually requires keying (roughening the surface so that the paint will adhere) and washing. To key the existing paint, brush away any dust and wipe with trisodium phosphate (TSP) on a sponge. This will reveal any cracks that require filling (*see opposite*). If there are no cracks, dry the surface with a lint-free cloth. If you cannot obtain TSP, key the surface with medium-to-fine grain sandpaper.

KEY THE SURFACE WITH TSP

6 REMOVING FLAKING PAINT

If a painted surface is in poor condition and the paint is flaking, you will have to strip it off before repainting. Use a wide-bladed scraper to remove the paint. If the paint is stubborn, apply a chemical stripper. When the surface is bare, smooth it with medium-grain sandpaper wrapped around a cork block. If the surface has been painted with tempera, seal it with a stabilizing solution after you have sanded it down.

SAND THE STRIPPED SURFACE

7 HOW TO FILL HOLES

It is worth filling even small cracks and holes for a professional result. You can buy filler as ready-mixed paste or as a powder that must be mixed before use. Always check manufacturers' instructions before preparing the paste. The average drying time is 30 minutes. Fill large holes with several layers of filler if necessary. After filling, sand down the surface. Filler can be difficult to remove from equipment, so if you are mixing your own, line the container with a plastic bag to avoid a messy cleaning job afterward.

1 Start by brushing away loose debris with a small decorating brush.

2 Wet the hole with a small, damp brush to ensure that the filler stays inside the hole.

3 Press the filler into hole with a putty knife. Allow filler to dry between layers. Wipe off excess.

4 Smooth with the wet blade of a putty knife. Once dry, sand with fine-grain sandpaper.

8 PREPARING PAINT

Once a can of paint has been opened, dirt may contaminate it or a skin may form on the surface. To prevent any contamination, always replace the lid after use and store the can upside down.

1 ▷ To prevent debris on the can surface from falling into the paint, brush the rim with a paintbrush.

2 Work around the rim of the lid with the blunt edge of a flat-bladed knife, prying the lid until it springs open.

3 Stir the paint with a piece of wooden doweling in wide and narrow circles to give a consistent color.

9 WHY USE A PAINT BUCKET?

It makes sense to work out of a paint bucket rather than a paint can. It will enable you to transfer as much paint as you need at one time, and a bucket with a handle can be hung from a ladder. Once you have mixed the paint, pour as much as you need into the bucket. Line the bucket with aluminum foil before you fill it, as paint can be difficult to remove. Place the foil with the shiny surface up.

FOIL-LINED BUCKET

10 WHEN TO SIEVE PAINT

Sieve paint if you see bits of debris in it, or if a skin has formed. A just-opened new can does not need to be sieved.

1 Use a knife to cut around the top skin. Remove the skin by carefully pulling it to one side of the can.

2 Stretch muslin or old nylon hose across the bucket and pour the paint through. Store the paint in an airtight jar.

11 PAINTBRUSH KNOW-HOW

For large areas use a wide brush or roller. Tackle intricate areas with an artist's brush. A range of in-between brush sizes is available.

1 Use only new brushes for priming as they may shed bristles. To remove debris, flick the brush against your hand.

2 Dip a third of the bristle length into the paint. Dab the bristles against the bucket side to remove any excess paint.

PAINTING WALLS & CEILINGS

12 ORDER OF WORK

Remove the furniture and wall hangings or place them in the center of the room, and cover with a dropcloth. Remove light fixtures from the walls if possible, and cover outlets with plastic bags. Cover the floor with a dropcloth. Now clean and prepare the surfaces to be painted. The ceiling should be the starting point, then work across the walls. Paint the woodwork last.

Paint away from main light source

Begin by painting the ceiling

13 HOW TO APPLY LATEX PAINT

Ideal for walls and ceilings, latex is available as a matte or silk finish. It is water soluble and dries quickly.

1 △ Work in areas of 2 sq ft (60 sq cm) in light, crisscross strokes. Do not apply the paint too thickly.

2 Finish with an upward stroke. Move to the adjacent area. Do not apply more coats until the first coat is dry.

14 BEADING

Making a well-defined line between two colors in a corner – for example, where walls meet a ceiling – is known as beading. Wait until the paint on the ceiling is dry, and then holding the brush parallel to, but a short distance away from, the ceiling, press it against the wall, splaying the bristles. This will create a bead of paint that should be pushed steadily into the edge or corner. Work across the wall.

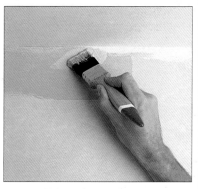

BEADING AT THE CEILING

15 CUTTING IN

Painting the edges around a window or door frame before the rest of the wall is known as cutting in. Once all the edges have been painted in this way, deal with the remainder of the room, blending in the fresh paint with the edges.

1 △ With a small brush, carefully paint narrow strips, about 1–2 in (2.5–5 cm) wide, at right angles to the frame. Leave a very small gap between the painted strips and the edge of the door frame.

2 Paint over the strips of color with a line parallel to the frame. Make sure to run the bristles close to the edge of the frame to create a well-defined line.

16 PAINTING WITH A ROLLER

Rollers are useful for painting large areas and are available in different sizes and textures. Foam and mohair sleeves are good for covering smooth surfaces; wood and deep-pile synthetic suit rough surfaces. Cut in edges before using on a wall (*see p.15*).

1 △ Rollers are suitable for applying latex paint: oil-based paint can be difficult to clean off from the cover. Prepare for painting by pouring a quantity of paint into a clean, dry roller tray.

2 Place the roller sleeve over the roller. Dip the roller in the paint, rolling it up and down the incline of the tray until it is well covered.

3 Apply the paint randomly by running the roller up and down the wall and from side to side. Spread the paint as evenly as possible, and try not to let the roller slide across the wall.

4 To complete one area, lift off in an upward stroke. When you move to an adjacent area, roll over the wet edges to blend. Be careful not to splash paint onto the woodwork.

17 WHEN TO USE A PAINT PAD

Paint pads are interchangeable with rollers. They are ideal for applying water-based paint to large areas. Although they can be used with oil-based paints, it is possible that the cleaning solvents required to remove oil-based paint could damage the sponge. Paint pads can be used to paint metalwork and wood.

1 △ Pour the paint into a paint-pad tray or a roller tray. Lightly dip the pad into the paint, keeping the pad flat. Do not submerge it. If overloaded, wipe off the excess. Alternatively, buy an applicator to apply paint to the pad.

2 Cover the surface randomly in a light, crisscross motion. Do not press too hard or the paint will drip. Reload the pad only when you can see that the paint coverage is beginning to thin.

18 HOW TO PAINT A CEILING

You can paint a ceiling working from a stepladder or a work platform (make sure yours is stable) or from the floor using a roller or paint pad with a handle extension. If you are standing on a platform, leave at least 3 in (7.5 cm) above your head. Divide the ceiling into sections of about 1–1½ ft (30–45 cm) wide and work each section away from the main light source.

A ROLLER WITH AN EXTENSION

19 Using Masking Tape

If you intend to divide an area horizontally into two colors or to paint around an object such as a switchplate, it is helpful to stick down low-tack masking tape to create a straight line between the different color divisions. You can use tape along the edge of the floor to keep it free of paint when you decorate the baseboards. Also use masking tape to attach stencils to a wall (see pp.36–37).

MASKING TAPE

1 Mark the line between the two colors with a soft pencil and a ruler. Check the alignment of the horizontal line with a level and the vertical line with a level or plumb line.

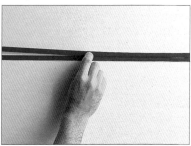

2 Stick down the masking tape along the line, making sure that the pencil line is still visible. If your dividing line is vertical, stick the masking tape along the far edge of the line.

3 Apply paint from the middle of the masking tape downward with a small decorating brush. Once you have covered the immediate area, paint the rest of the surface with a large brush.

4 When you have finished painting the wall and the paint is completely dry, you can pull off the tape. The use of low-tack masking tape keeps the paint from being peeled off at the same time.

20 PAINTING OUTLET COVERS

Switchplates can be removed from the wall, but if you do this, you must turn off the power supply first. To take off the cover, ease the plate from the surface with a screwdriver or flat-bladed knife. Then carefully paint behind the surround. An easier option is to paint around the cover. To do this, stick masking tape around the edges.

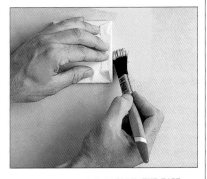

CAREFULLY PAINT AROUND THE TAPE

21 ADDING DETAILS

Wooden and plaster details, such as moldings, cornices, and dado rails, should be painted with a small decorating brush or artist's brush. Paint the background color with a 1-in (25-mm) brush and then pick out the fine details with an artist's brush. Keep your hand steady on a maulstick as you paint. Use masking tape (see opposite) to keep a straight line between two colors.

REST YOUR HAND ON A MAULSTICK

22 PAINT SAFELY

Safety is a real issue; always read the manufacturers' labels before you begin decorating, and wear the necessary protective clothing.
- Many of the solvents used to clean painting tools give off toxic fumes, so make sure that your work area is well ventilated.
- Mineral spirits, methylated spirits, and turpentine are dangerous if inhaled, swallowed, or allowed to come into contact with the skin.
- It is advisable not to eat, drink, or smoke while painting.
- Keep paint and cleaning agents away from children and pets.
- Wear a dust mask when working with powder colors.
- Since some paints and cleaning agents can irritate the skin, it is a good idea to wear protective gloves.
- If painting overhead, wear goggles and stand on a secure, level base.

PAINTING WOOD

23 HOW TO PREPARE BARE WOOD

Plan ahead when painting wood; it may need several coats of oil-based paint. Lightly sand any rough areas and wipe away the dust with a lint-free cloth dampened in turpentine. Seal knots with shellac or knotting. When dry, apply a layer of primer. When that dries, sand lightly, and then apply a couple of layers of undercoat.

Knotting *Primer* *Undercoat* *Topcoat*

24 HOW TO PAINT BARE WOOD

Wood is usually painted with oil-based paint. This gives off toxic fumes, so always keep the room well ventilated. When the undercoat is dry, sand and wipe. Apply one or two topcoats for a good finish.

1 Hold a small brush like a pen and apply vertical, parallel lines of paint. Work in sections 1 sq ft (30 sq cm).

2 Without reloading the brush with paint, join the vertical lines by brushing across them with horizontal strokes.

3 Finish with more vertical strokes. Reload the brush before starting on the next area. Begin by the wet edge.

25 REPAINTING WOODWORK

Wash and sand old, painted woodwork before repainting. If the paint is in a bad condition, it is best to strip it off before repainting.

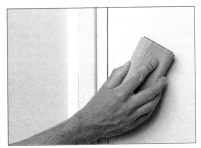

1 Wash with TSP. If rough, sand using medium sandpaper. Wipe with lint-free cloth dampened in turpentine.

2 Paint the topcoat onto the clean surface. For a different color, apply an undercoat, let it dry, and repaint.

26 SMOOTHING BETWEEN COATS

As you paint, small bristles, dust particles, and other debris will inevitably become caught in the wet, painted surface. Check the surface after each coat. If you spot blemishes, sand the surface between coats.

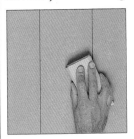

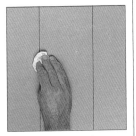

1 When dry, inspect the area for blemishes. Smooth the area, using fine sandpaper wrapped around a cork block.

2 To check that all the bumps have been removed, rub the palm of your hand over the surface. Brush away any dust.

3 To remove any last traces of dust, rub the area with a piece of damp, lint-free cloth. When the surface is dry, repaint.

27 PAINTING BETWEEN ROOMS

To paint a door and frame between two rooms in different colors, follow this procedure: open the door and stand in one room (marked A on the picture). Paint the lock edge, the adjacent edge of the frame, the doorstop, and the door front. Open the door wide so that the hinge is visible and stand in the other room (marked B on the picture). In the second color, paint the hinge edge, the flat of the doorstop, and the door front.

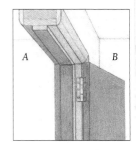

PAINTING IN TWO COLORS

28 HOW TO VARNISH WOOD

Unpainted and painted woods benefit from a couple of coats of varnish. Varnish protects against wear and tear. It is available in gloss, semi-gloss, and matte finishes. To change the color of the wood, use a pigmented varnish. Prepare as you would for oil-based paint (see p.20).

1 Pour some varnish into a bucket and dip a lint-free cloth into it. Rub the varnish into the wood, working against the grain. Wait for the varnish to dry (up to 12 hours).

2 Lightly rub the surface with fine sandpaper wrapped around a cork block. Wipe dust particles off the surface with a lint-free cloth that has been dampened in turpentine.

3 Apply another coat of varnish using a clean brush. When the varnish has dried, lightly sand the surface down and wipe clean. The results should be smooth and dust-free.

29 PROCEDURE FOR DOORS

The best way to paint a door is to start at the top and work down. Paint the main part of the door with a 2 or 3 in (50 or 75 mm) brush.

The frame and details should be painted with a smaller brush. Follow the numbered sequence below, painting the frame last.

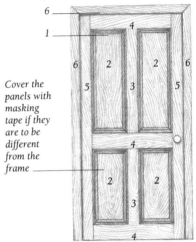

Start at the top and work down

Paint the frame with a smaller brush

Cover the panels with masking tape if they are to be different from the frame

PAINTING FLUSH DOORS
Start at the top of the door, working down in narrow horizontal bands, making sure that the adjoining edges blend well.

PAINTING PANELED DOORS
Paint the moldings first, then the panels, and then the frame, and finish off with the door opening.

30 HOW TO PAINT BASEBOARDS

Baseboards take a lot of abuse, so protect them with a durable finish such as oil-based paint. To protect the floor, lay down a strip of masking tape or slide a cardboard mask under the baseboard. To protect the wall, hold the cardboard mask on top of the baseboard. Paint with horizontal strokes using a 2 in (50 mm) brush. Apply a couple of coats of varnish.

CARDBOARD PROTECTS FLOOR

31 PROCEDURE FOR WINDOWS

Paint windows early in the day, or you may have to leave them open all night to dry. Oil-based paints take several hours to dry. Stick masking tape around the edges of the glass, leaving a ¹⁄₁₆ in (2 mm) gap between the frame and window; paint will overlap onto the glass, protecting the frame against water damage.

CASEMENT WINDOWS ▷
In order, paint the rebates and crossbars (1), crossrails (2), hinge edge and hanging stile (3), meeting stile (4), and frame (5).

Leave metal locks bare or paint them black

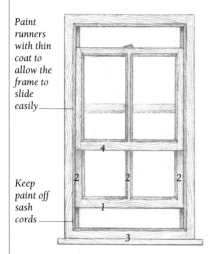

Paint runners with thin coat to allow the frame to slide easily

Keep paint off sash cords

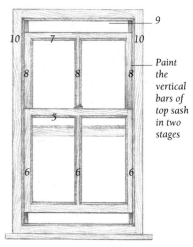

Paint the vertical bars of top sash in two stages

PAINTING SASH WINDOWS
Reverse the top and bottom frames. Paint the meeting rail (1), vertical bars (2), lower runners and frame (3), crossrail and underside (4). Once dry, reverse the frames. Paint a crossrail (5), vertical bars (6), other crossrail (7), remainder (8), soffit, upper runners, behind cord (9), frame (10).

32 REMEDY FAULTS

Keep equipment and paint clean to minimize the risk of paint faults. Surfaces should be clean, dry, and dust-free. Paint should be fresh or sieved and always applied to a compatible undercoat. Keep paint can lids well sealed. To close a can, place a piece of wood over the lid and hammer it shut. Store brushes, paint pads, and rollers in a dry place, wrapped in lint-free cloth or paper.

DARKENED AREAS
Scrape off the affected area, sand, apply knotting, and recoat when dry.

TEARS & RUNS
Let the paint dry. Rub with sandpaper, clean off the dust, and then recoat.

WRINKLING
Occurs when paint is applied before first coat is dry. Strip and recoat.

GRIT
If grit is embedded in dry paint, sand lightly, brush, and wipe off when dry.

BLISTERING
Strip paint (if open-grained wood, fill), prime, undercoat, and then repaint.

POOR COVERAGE
If the undercoat shows through, apply another layer of latex paint.

FLAKING
Surface was not properly prepared. Strip, prepare surface, and repaint.

STAINING
Coat the painted surface with an aluminum primer sealer and repaint.

CRAZING
Occurs when paints are incompatible. Strip and prepare surface. Repaint.

INSECTS
In dry paint, sand and recoat the area. In wet paint, brush off and touch up.

PAINT EFFECTS

33 EFFECTS EQUIPMENT

Creating textured surfaces is an easy form of paint decoration. Some of the equipment, such as the rag used for ragging, is everyday; some, such as whitewashing wax, is specialized.

FLOGGER

SOFTENER

STENCIL BRUSH

SHORT-HAIRED DECORATING BRUSH

POWDERED WHITING

LINSEED OIL

TURPENTINE

DRIER

LARGE DECORATING BRUSH

△ GLAZE INGREDIENTS
One of the simplest paint effects to achieve is to soften paintwork by adding a glaze.

BRONZE-WIRE HANDBRUSH

STIPPLER

△ BRUSHES
Depending on the effect, use a stiff or soft brush. Some are used to fleck, some to stab.

PLASTIC BAG

LINT-FREE CLOTH

ARTIST'S OIL COLOR

POWDER COLORS

WHITE-WASHING WAX

△ CLOTHS & SPONGES
A wide variety of textured effects can be achieved using rags, sponges, and bags.

SPONGE

△ PIGMENTS & WAXES
Use pigment to put color into glazes. Whitewashing wax colors grained wood.

34 HOW TO MAKE A TINTED OIL GLAZE

Applying a tinted oil glaze to a surface is an excellent way of both softening and complementing the underlying color. Buy a transparent glaze from a paint store and add color or make your own glaze.

INGREDIENTS FOR 1 QUART (1 LITER)
Mix 2½ cups (0.6 liters) turpentine, 1¼ cups (0.3 liters) boiled linseed oil, ¾ cup (0.2 liters) driers, and 1 tbsp whiting.

ADD COLOR
Mix mineral spirits and color to the desired tone. Add glaze a little at a time. Put in more color and mineral spirits for the right tone.

35 APPLYING A GLAZE

Apply a glaze to a matte oil-painted surface. When dry, cover with a coat or two of varnish. You can work on a glaze from ½–1 hour. Prepare a smooth surface, and coat with two layers of semigloss paint.

1 Apply the glaze with a decorating brush randomly over an area of 1 sq yd (1 sq m) at a time.

2 Use a wide, short-bristled decorating brush to spread the glaze as evenly as possible.

3 Use a softening brush to smooth the glaze. If necessary, wipe the bristles on lint-free cloth.

36 SPONGING ON

This technique gives a soft, mottled appearance to a surface. It is achieved by dabbing tinted oil glaze onto a surface with a sponge – preferably a quality natural sponge. You can apply several different colored glazes, depending on the desired final look.

NATURAL SPONGE

▽ THE EFFECT
A soft, sponged effect in the bathroom helps create a soothing and relaxing atmosphere.

1 Prepare the surface with a couple of coats of matte oil-based paint. Allow the undercoat to dry. Pour the glaze into a roller tray, and immerse a sponge in it.

To remove any excess glaze, press the sponge against the slope of the tray. If you are not sure of how soaked the sponge should be, experiment on cardboard.

Dab the sponge onto the wall to create a dappled look. Vary the pressure for effect. Be quite free in the way you apply the glaze. Squeeze any excess glaze onto a lint-free cloth. Seal with matte varnish.

37 SPONGING OFF

The finished effect creates a more opaque color than that made by sponging on. Prepare by applying two coats of a matte oil-based paint.

1 Mix the oil glaze to the texture of thick cream. Paint in small areas of 6 ft (2 m) by 3 ft (1 m) so that the glaze does not dry before you sponge it off.

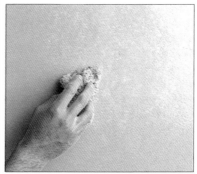

2 Soak the sponge in turpentine. Then wring it out and dab it onto the wet tinted oil glaze to remove some of the paint. The more paint you remove, the lighter the finished effect.

29

38 DRAGGING

Smooth the surface and then cover with one or two coats of matte oil-based paint. Next, apply the tinted oil glaze over the matte paint in vertical strips 2 ft (60 cm) wide. When the glaze is applied, take a flogger brush and drag it down the wall in vertical strokes. The color of the matte paint will show through the glaze. As you work, wipe off the excess glaze from the brush with a lint-free cloth. Use the brush firmly.

DRAG THE FLOGGER DOWN THE WALL

39 RAGGING

Ragging creates an indistinct patterned effect. Apply a coat of matte oil-based paint to a prepared surface. Brush on the glaze. Bunch up a lint-free cloth and dab off the glaze from the surface. After 30 minutes, brush over with the tip of a softening brush to soften.

△ THE OVERALL EFFECT OF RAGGING
Ragging creates a very subtle effect. The color and pattern on a finished surface should look like a soft blur.

◁ SOFTENING THE EFFECT
With ragging you soften the color twice, first with a lint-free cloth and second with the tips of a softening brush.

40 RAG-ROLLING

Rolling a lint-free cloth over a properly prepared wall will give it a randomly distressed look. First prepare the surface and then apply a coat of matte oil-based paint. As it is vital to work quickly, the tinted oil glaze should be applied with a wide decorating brush to small areas. You will need several lint-free cloths or just one chamois leather.

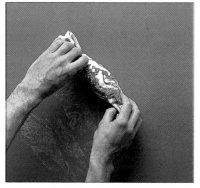

1 Dip the lint-free cloth or chamois leather into turpentine. Wring the cloth out and roll it up. Then lightly roll the cloth over the tinted oil glaze.

2 Keep rolling the rag in different directions to create a distressed effect. Once the lint-free cloth is covered with paint, replace it with a fresh one.

41 BAGGING

This technique creates a strong, textured look. Prepare the surface with a coat of matte oil-based paint, and working in sections of approximately 2 sq yds (2 sq m), paint on the tinted oil glaze. Place a rolled-up cloth in a plastic bag and run the bag over the surface in a pattern, such as overlapping circles. Wipe off any excess glaze from the bag. When the glaze is dry, protect it with a layer of matte varnish.

CREATE PATTERNS WITH A BAG

42 STIPPLING

To create a stippled effect, you need a special tool known as a stippling brush. Prepare by painting the surface with a coat of matte oil-based paint and mixing the tinted oil glaze to a creamlike consistency.

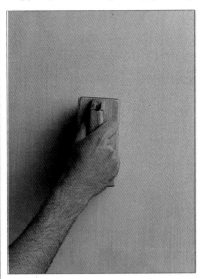

1 Work in areas of 1 sq yd (1 sq m). Stab at the wall with the stippling brush to create a mottled effect. Try not to slide the brush across the wall.

2 ▽ To create an even coverage you may need to overlap at adjacent areas. When necessary, wipe off the glaze from the brush with a lint-free cloth.

43 STORE-BOUGHT TEXTURED PAINT

A light, textured look can be created with a cut-foam roller and store-bought textured paint. Prepare the surface with a suitable undercoat. Roll the textured paint onto the wall with broad, overlapping strokes. Most store-bought textured paint is white, so if you want to add some color, wait until the paint is dry and then apply a coat of colored latex. The texture will still show through.

ROLLING ON TEXTURED PAINT

44 GLAZING YOUR WALLS

By glazing, or colorwashing, a wall, you will create a dappled surface texture, similar to that of tempera ("distemper"). First prepare the wall with a coat of opaque latex paint and then paint over with thinned latex.

DAPPLED COLOR ▷
Glazing creates a similar effect to tempera. It works particularly well on uneven surfaces, such as cracked plaster, where it creates a highly textured look.

1 Thin the latex paint; the ratio of latex to water varies depending on the type of paint. Experiment with ratios 4:1 to 9:1 latex to water. Apply in small areas of 1 sq yd (1 sq m). Run over with a damp brush to soften the strokes.

2 Apply the second coat once the first is completely dry. Paint the second coat as the first, with a wide decorating brush in small areas. If the paint runs, keep brushing it. When dry, finish with a coat of matte varnish to protect the surface.

45 GLAZING WOOD

Strip and sand the wood to prepare for glazing (see p.20). Dilute a quantity of latex so that it penetrates beneath the surface of the wood. Test the diluted paint on a small area to check the consistency.

1 Apply the diluted paint freely with a large decorating brush. Brush in the direction of the grain, covering the wood in small areas at a time.

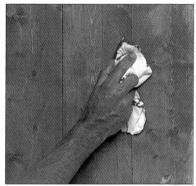

2 When the paint is nearly dry (test an area), gently wipe over the paint with a lint-free cloth in one direction to expose the underlying wood grain.

3 Leave the paint to dry overnight and check that you like the tone. If it is too weak, apply another coat. Follow by sanding with fine sandpaper.

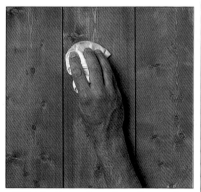

4 The final stage is to clean the wood. Run across the surface with a dry decorating brush and afterward wipe over with a damp cloth.

46 PICKLING WOOD

Pickling, or liming, enhances wooden surfaces by giving them a soft white tone and revealing the wood grain. For this technique you need liming paste or wax, clear-paste wax, a wire brush, and steel wool.

1 Before applying the liming paste or wax, you need to open the grain of the wood. Rub the wood with a wire brush in the direction of the grain.

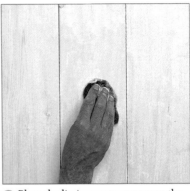

2 Place the liming paste or wax on the steel wool and rub it into the wood grain using a circular motion. Work in areas of about ½ sq yd (½ sq m) at a time.

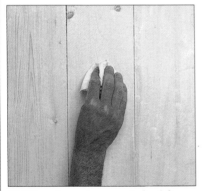

3 When the paste or wax is dry (after several minutes), rub on a fine, clear-paste wax with a lint-free cloth to remove the excess. Buff with a lint-free cloth.

PICKLED BATH PANELING
Pickling gives wood a mellow appearance and emphasizes the grain beneath.

47 STENCILING

This is a simple way of applying repeat patterns to walls, floors, and furniture. Make a stencil from either acetate or stencil cardboard and apply the color with a stencil brush. Stencil the whole area or just a border, such as a frieze.

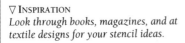

READY-MADE STENCILS
Instead of making your own stencils, choose from the wealth of ready-made stencil designs that are available in most art stores.

▽ **INSPIRATION**
Look through books, magazines, and at textile designs for your stencil ideas.

1 When you choose a stencil design, consider how many colors you want as each will require a separate stencil. Transfer the chosen design onto a piece of tracing paper with a soft pencil.

△ **STENCIL EFFECTS**
Use stencils to cover a whole wall area, like wallpaper, or to create special effects such as a dado rail and cornice.

2 Turn over the tracing paper and stick it face down onto a piece of cardboard with some masking tape. Using a medium-hard pencil, draw over the reverse of the design so that the image is rubbed onto the cardboard.

3 Place the cardboard on a cutting mat. Pierce it with a craft knife, and then pull the cardboard toward the blade. You may need to create bridges to hold the pattern in place (for example, if your design contains a circle within a circle).

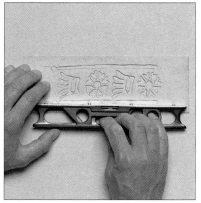

4 Mark where you want the image to go on your wall with a pencil. If you are creating a frieze, use a level to find the true horizontal. Secure the stencil cardboard in place with low-tack tape.

5 Dip the stencil brush into the paint and wipe off any excess. Apply with a stabbing action. Be careful not to allow excess paint to drip off the cardboard onto the wall. Use any paint for this effect.

PREPARING TO WALLPAPER

48 WHY WALLPAPER?

Hanging wallpaper is an easy way of creating a regular pattern or color over a surface in just one layer. Wallpaper comes in a wide variety of colors, patterns, and materials. Modern wallpapers are more durable than those of the past, and many are washable. Hanging lining paper is a very effective means of covering cracked or uneven surfaces prior to wallpapering.

DECORATIVE BORDER

49 HOW MANY ROLLS?

Use the chart to work out the number of standard-size rolls (measuring 33 ft (10 m) long and 21 in (530 mm) wide) required. For other sizes, check the manufacturer's charts for the number needed.

Wallpaper	Distance around room (including doors and windows)						
	33 ft	39 ft	46 ft	52 ft	59 ft	66 ft	72 ft
Wall height	10 m	12 m	14 m	16 m	18 m	20 m	22 m
7 ft–7 ft 6 in (2.1–2.3 m)	5	5	6	7	8	9	10
7 ft 6 in–8 ft (2.3–2.4 m)	5	6	7	8	9	10	10
8 ft–8 ft 6 in (2.4–2.6 m)	5	6	7	9	10	11	12
8 ft 6 in–9 ft (2.6–2.7 m)	5	6	7	9	10	11	12
9 ft–9 ft 6 in (2.7–2.9 m)	6	7	8	9	10	12	12

Ceiling Paper	Distance around room						
feet	30–40	42–50	55–60	65–70	75–80	85–90	95–100
meters	9–12	13–15	17–18	20–21	23–24	26–27	29–30
Number of rolls	2	3	4	6	7	9	10

50 PAPERING EQUIPMENT

Wallpapering requires advance planning, so have your equipment ready. Besides the equipment below, trash bags are useful for disposing of trimmed wallpaper.

HOUSEHOLD BROOM

STEAM STRIPPER **SPONGE**

PASTING BRUSH **SMOOTHING BRUSH**

△ **BROOM & BRUSHES**
A broom helps hold paper up, and a paper-hanging brush smooths hung paper.

WALLPAPER SCISSORS **SEAM ROLLER**

LEVEL

PLUMB LINE **MATCHSTICKS** **STEEL TAPE**

WOODEN DOWELING **CRAFT KNIFE**

△ **MISCELLANEOUS EQUIPMENT**
Use a sponge to wipe off excess paste and wooden doweling to stir paste and size.

△ **MEASURING & MARKING**
These will help you align the wallpaper correctly. Matchsticks make good markers.

WATER TRAY

ADHESIVE

PASTING TABLE

LADDER

BUCKET WITH HANDLE **VINYL ADHESIVE** **SIZE**

△ **ADHESIVES & CONTAINERS**
Mix paste and size in a bucket. Use a water tray to soak ready-pasted paper.

LADDERS & TABLES △
It is very important to work from a secure ladder at the right height. The pasting table should also be level and stable.

51 HOW TO REMOVE OLD WALLPAPER

New wallpaper should be hung on a smooth surface, ideally on top of lining paper. If the old wallpaper is in good condition, you can hang the new over it. However, old washable, vinyl, relief, or metal (foil) wallpaper must be removed.

Before stripping off old paper, take down shelving, pictures, curtains, and blinds, but leave switchplates and hooks in place. Once you have stripped the old paper, wipe and lightly scrape the surface again to remove all traces of the old glue.

1 Score the old paper using the sharp edge of a scraper. Do not use a knife to cut into the paper as you may damage the wall beneath. Cover the entire surface area in score marks.

2 If you wet the scored paper, it will rise away from the wall. Divide the wall into sections and soak the old wallpaper of each section using a sponge and warm water.

3 After a minute or so, the wallpaper should easily come away from the wall. Scrape off the paper. Once you have removed the paper, lightly scrape the wall to remove any traces of glue.

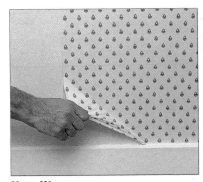

VINYL WALLPAPER
This is easily removed by carefully peeling each length of paper off the wall.

52 STEAM STRIPPING

If you have a large area of wallpaper to remove, use a steam stripper. These come in various sizes and can be rented from hardware stores. With a steam stripper, you do not need to sponge the wallpaper. Score the old wallpaper with the sharp edge of a scraper, and then hold the steam stripper against the surface. As the paper begins to loosen, scrape it off with a wallpaper scraper.

STEAM STRIP OLD WALLPAPER

53 SIZING SURFACES

Before hanging wallpaper, prepare the wall surface with a coat of size. Consult the manufacturer's instructions to make sure you buy a size that is compatible with the type of wallpaper you have chosen. Apply with a large, clean decorating brush to a dry wall. If any size splashes onto the woodwork, quickly wipe it off with a damp cloth.

APPLY SIZE TO A PREPARED SURFACE

54 MIXING PASTE

The paper manufacturer will specify the type of paste you should use. Following the manufacturer's instructions, fill a bucket with cold water and add the paste powder. Mix the paste and water with a piece of wooden doweling. Some types of paste should be left to stand awhile.

MIX PASTE THOROUGHLY

41

55 ORDER OF WORK

Paint the ceiling and then the woodwork. Hang lining paper on the ceiling if the surface is poor. Next do the walls. Mark a vertical line from the ceiling to floor as a guide for aligning the first length of paper. Hang the lining paper. Work away from the main light source. Finish at a corner, near a door, where a mismatch will not be too obvious.

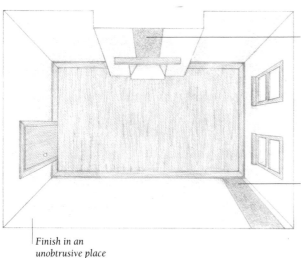

If you are using large-patterned paper, begin at the room's focal point, for example, above a fireplace

For small-patterned, striped, or plain wallpapers, begin on the longest wall nearest a light source and hang the lengths away from the light

Finish in an unobtrusive place

56 WHY HANG LINING PAPER?

Lining paper is used to cover up uneven surfaces on both walls and ceilings prior to wallpapering or painting. It is available in different grades of thickness. Woodchip paper, though not true lining paper, is very strong and can be used to cover walls that are in very poor condition. The thicker grades of lining paper are more suitable for hanging on ceilings.

- If you plan a paint finish, choose white lining paper.
- Use lightweight lining paper for nonabsorbent surfaces.
- Medium-weight lining paper is best for normal surfaces.
- Select heavyweight lining paper as a base for thick wallpaper or vinyl.
- Use brown lining paper as a base for very heavy coverings such as flocked wallpaper.

57 PLANNING AHEAD

It is vital that you work out a schedule before you begin. In particular, remember that you will have to wait until the lining paper is completely dry before you can start hanging the decorative wallpaper.

- Lining paper can take up to 12 hours to dry, so do not start hanging the wallpaper too soon.
- Make sure that you buy a suitable lining paper for the requirements of the surface. It is advisable to check the manufacturer's instructions.
- Make sure that you use a size and paste that are compatible with the recommended adhesive for the decorative wallpaper (see p.57).

Hang lining paper parallel to a window or main light source

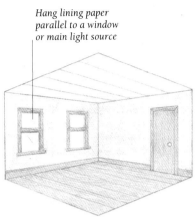

△ LINING CEILINGS
If the ceiling is in very poor condition, hang two layers of lining paper. Hang the second layer at right angles to the first.

Horizontal hanging keeps seams from aligning with wallpaper seams

Start from ceiling and work down

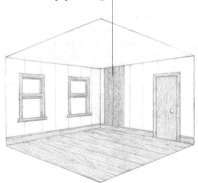

△ HORIZONTAL STRIPS
When hanging lining paper horizontally, begin at the ceiling and work downward to the baseboard or floor.

Hang half-width of lining paper where first length of decorative wallpaper is to go

△ VERTICAL STRIPS
Avoid the seams of vertically hung lining paper and wallpaper coinciding by hanging a half-width of lining paper first.

58 MEASURING & CUTTING LINING PAPER

The first preparatory task is to measure and cut the lining paper for the ceiling. It is essential to take accurate measurements and cut carefully. You will need a chalk line to align the lengths properly. An assistant will make the task easier. You should use a ruler or straightedge for marking the measurements onto the lining paper.

1 Measure the paper width and subtract ⅜ in (1 cm). Mark this at each end of the ceiling. String the chalk line taut between the two points. Snap the chalk line against the ceiling to make a mark.

2 Measure the length of the ceiling along the chalk line. On a length of lining paper, near one edge of the paper, mark the length of the ceiling, adding 2 in (5 cm) on each end for the overhang.

3 Using a ruler or a straightedge, mark a cutting line across the whole width of the lining paper. Carefully cut along this guideline with a pair of long-bladed wallpaper scissors.

4 If the length of the ceiling remains constant along its width, use the first length as a measure for the remaining lengths of paper. If not, take separate measurements and number each length.

59 HOW TO APPLY PASTE

The method for applying and spreading paste is the same for lining paper and wallpaper. Place the lining paper on the pasting table. The sides should overhang the table. Weigh down the paper.

1 Apply the paste to the center of the paper with a pasting brush in 3 ft (1 m) sections.

2 Spread the paste from the center toward the far edge. Use a generous amount of paste.

3 Once half a width is pasted, reload the brush and apply paste to the remaining side.

60 FOLDING THE PAPER LENGTHS

If you are working with a very long piece of paper, fold the paper after you have pasted it to make it more manageable. Always be careful not to crease the folds, because this will leave marks in the paper.

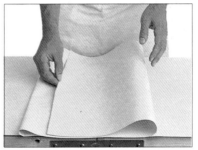

1 △ Fold the paper accordian-style about 1 ft (30 cm) wide, pasted side to pasted side. Do not crease the folds. Put the folds to one side and apply paste to the next section of the length of paper.

2 Continue pasting and folding along the whole length of the paper. Keep a short length unfolded at the end. This is the first section you will hang.

HANGING LINING PAPER

61 APPLYING CEILING PAPER

Assemble the work platform so that you leave a 3 in (7.5 cm) gap above your head. Build the scaffold to the same length as the paper. Place the platform directly below the chalk line (see p.44). Apply size to the first width of ceiling (see p.41). A broom is very useful to hold the paper up (an extra pair of hands is helpful). Hold the folded paper to the ceiling corner and align the long edge of the paper with the chalk mark.

1 Press the paper into the wall corner, leaving a 2 in (5 cm) overhang on the sides next to the walls.

2 Smooth the paper, release another fold, align it with the chalk mark, and smooth it from the center outward.

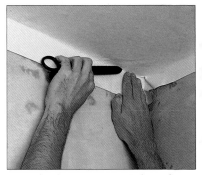

3 Carefully run the rounded tip of a pair of wallpaper scissors along the overhang to form a crease in the paper.

62 DEALING WITH THE OVERHANG

Once the lining paper is creased at the join of the wall to the ceiling, you can work on the overhang. Create neat corners or the covering paper will end up looking messy.

1 ▷ Cut a diagonal toward the ceiling corner. Overlap the ends to fit in the corner. Mark the crease with a pencil.

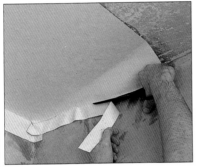

2 Pull the overhang away from the wall and ceiling. Cut along the pencil mark with a pair of wallpaper scissors.

3 Smooth back the paper with a paper-hanging brush. Repeat the procedure on the next width of ceiling.

63 SMOOTHING SEAMS

When you hang lining paper, make sure that the long edges of the lengths butt into each other. Once the paper is on the wall, smooth the seams between lengths with a seam roller. If there are any gaps, fill them with a flexible filler. You should do this once you have finished papering. Follow the manufacturer's instructions to apply the filler, and use a wide-bladed filler knife, which you can insert into the seam line.

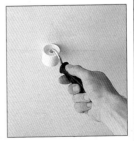

ROLL ALONG THE SEAM

64 WORKING AROUND ELECTRICAL FIXTURES

Safety is, of course, very important when you are working with electrical fixtures. Always turn off the electricity before applying size around a light fixture or switch. Before you begin, remove both the bulb and lamp and cover the electrical fixture with masking tape. The task will be easier if you have an assistant who can hold up the paper with a broom as you cut around the fixture. A pair of sharp scissors is also essential.

1 Paper over the fixture. Cut a cross in the paper over the fixture.

2 Carefully pull the light pendant through the hole. Smooth the paper with a paper-hanging brush, toward the fixture.

3 With a pair of sharp scissors, make a series of V-shaped cuts into the paper overhang around the electrical fixture.

4 Carefully cut around the overhang crease with a craft knife. Wipe off any excess paste with a damp cloth.

65 LINING WALLS

If you plan to hang wallpaper on top of the lining paper, hang the lining paper horizontally. Measure the walls, cut the paper, paste, and accordian-fold it into manageable lengths (see pp.44–45). Apply size to the wall (see p.41) and position the first length of paper adjacent to the ceiling. Unfold the paper section by section and slide it into place.

HORIZONTAL LENGTHS

HANGING WALLPAPER

66 MEASURING UP

Many decorative wallpapers are expensive, so when you buy the wallpaper, check that all the rolls are in the same dye lot. Measure the height of the wall from ceiling to baseboard and add 4 in (10 cm) for the top and bottom overhang. Lay the roll on the pasting table and unroll. Mark up the first length and cut out with wallpaper scissors (*see p.44*). If the walls are even, cut out several lengths at once.

67 MATCH PATTERNS

Turn the paper so that the pattern faces up. Match the paper pattern to align across the lengths. Remember to leave enough paper for the overhang. Number the length and on the back of the paper indicate the direction in which it will hang. When all the lengths are cut and numbered, put them aside. Take the first length and place it on the table with the pattern facing down. Apply the paste (*see p.45*).

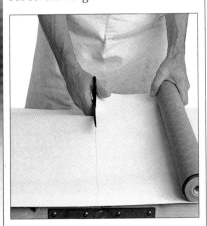

CUT WITH WALLPAPER SCISSORS

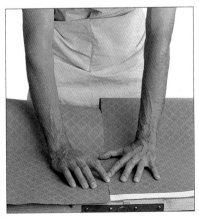

ALIGN THE PATTERN ACROSS LENGTHS

68 WHY FOLD PAPER?

Folding wallpaper is a way of making the lengths easier to work with, especially if they are very long. Make sure that you fold the paper without creasing it.

1 Fold the paper in 3 ft (1 m) sections. The pasted areas should lie adjacent to one another. Do not let paste stick to the decorative side.

2 To finish the process, leave a 28 in (70 cm) tongue of paper at the end of the bottom section of the length. Fold the tongue with the pasted sides together.

69 POSITIONING & SMOOTHING PAPER

Snap a chalk line against the wall to mark a vertical line for aligning the first length of wallpaper. Apply size to the wall.

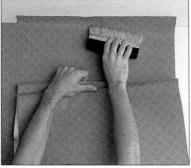

1 Guide the top edge of the paper to the ceiling, letting it overhang by 2 in (5 cm). Brush the paper from the center outward, smoothing it against the wall.

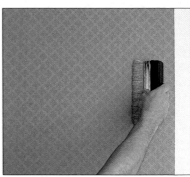

2 Unfold each accordian fold, smoothing the paper to the wall and aligning it to the plumb line mark. Allow the bottom tongue to hang folded.

70 THE TOP OVERHANG

To make the top and bottom edges of the wallpaper neat, follow these steps. If the ceiling has a non-washable finish, make the overhang smaller than the one below, to keep paste from soiling the ceiling.

1 At the join of the wall and ceiling, crease the wallpaper by running the rounded edge of a pair of scissors across it.

2 Gently pull away the top part of the paper and cut along the crease line. It may help if you mark the crease in pencil.

3 Using a paper-hanging brush, fit the top edge of the paper against the ceiling. Remove excess paste with a damp sponge.

71 THE BOTTOM OVERHANG

Unravel the accordian-folded paper, but be careful not to let the bottom tongue stick to the wall. To avoid this, keep the bottom tongue folded until you are ready to work with it.

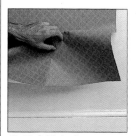

1 Unfold the bottom tongue of paper. Align the bottom edge so that it is parallel to the baseboard or floor.

2 Push the paper into the edge of the baseboard. Crease the overhang and cut it off. Brush the paper in place.

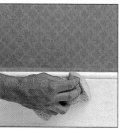

3 Wipe off the excess paste with a damp sponge. As you work across the wall, secure the edges with a seam roller.

72 PAPERING EXTERNAL CORNERS

Papering around an external corner is not as difficult as it may first appear. Hang the paper length so that it reaches slightly beyond the corner and then paste a cut-off piece of wallpaper over it. If you are using vinyl paper, apply vinyl adhesive to the overhang. It is always best to hide the cut piece on a part of the wall you don't see.

1 Carefully ease the wallpaper around the external corner using a paper-hanging brush, but do not smooth it down.

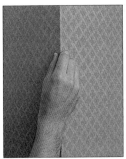

2 Run a finger and thumb down the corner to crease it. Mark a line from ceiling to floor 1 in (2.5 cm) from the corner.

3 Cut through the wallpaper along the line with a sharp craft knife. Guide the craft knife with a straightedge.

4 Carefully ease away the cut width of wallpaper. You will use this later, so put it aside on the pasting table.

5 Smooth the overhang with a seam roller. Apply more size to the wall and extra paste to the cut piece.

6 Paste the cut piece onto the wall. Try to match the pattern. Smooth the paper with a brush and the seam with a roller.

73 PAPERING INTERNAL CORNERS

Papering around an internal corner presents similar problems as for an external corner. Hang the paper slightly beyond the corner and then paste a cut-off piece over the overhang. The first vertical line must be straight. Check it with a level. If the first line is not true, you may carry the fault all the way around the rest of the room.

1 Measure from the last width of paper into the internal corner, adding 1 in (2.5 cm). Cut out a piece of paper this width.

2 Hang the cut length so that it aligns with and adjoins the last width of paper. Smooth the paper into the internal corner.

3 Run a roller up and down the overhang so that it is stuck onto the wall. Quickly wipe the paste from the roller.

4 Measure the width of the cut-off piece and add ¼ in (5 mm). From the corner, measure it at points down the wall.

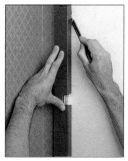

5 Place a level against the pencil marks to check that they form a true vertical line. Apply paste to the cut piece.

6 Align the outer edge of the cut piece against the vertical line. Use this line as a starting point for the rest of the room.

53

74 PAPERING AROUND FIXTURES

You may leave switchplates and outlets in place and paper around them. Matchsticks are useful for marking screw holes. Take out the fixture and put a matchstick into its place. Hang wallpaper over the matchstick, which you should press through the paper. When the paper is dry, remove the matchstick and put back the fixture.

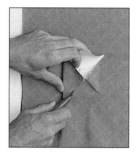

1 Switch off the electricity and cover the fixture with masking tape before applying size. Once the area is papered, make a firm outline of the fixture with a brush.

2 Use a sharp craft knife to cut away the paper from the center of the fixture to its corners with diagonal cuts. Carefully peel back the flaps of paper from the switch.

3 Cut off the paper flaps with a craft knife. Smooth the paper around the switch plate with a paper-hanging brush. Wipe off any paste before turning on the power.

75 PAPERING BEHIND FIXTURES

Begin by repeating steps 1 and 2 (*above*). Ease away the plate. Use an insulated electrical screwdriver to loosen the bolts. Leave a gap of ¼ in (5 mm) between the wall and plate. Carefully press the wallpaper behind the plate and smooth it down with a paper-hanging brush. Push the plate back into place and wipe off any paste. Never use this method if the wallpaper contains metal.

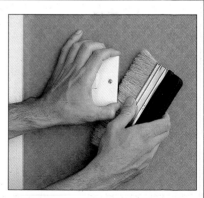

SMOOTH THE PAPER BEHIND THE PLATE

76 PAPERING AROUND FRAMES

To paper around a door or window, you need to cut pieces of wallpaper to fit around the frame. When measuring the wallpaper, always allow for the paper to overhang by approximately 1¼ in (3 cm). Apply size to the wall and push a length of pasted wallpaper into the join between the wall and the frame. Smooth the wallpaper over the wood with your fingers so that you form a clear outline of the molding. If the paste begins to dry as you work, keep applying more.

1 Smooth the wallpaper into the join with a paper-hanging brush.

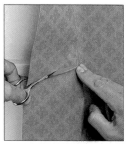

2 Cut into the wallpaper, carefully following the outline of the molding.

3 Cut away until you can fit the paper around the first rung of molding.

4 Make several small cuts toward the next rung of molding.

5 Press the paper into the edge around the frame with your fingers.

6 Pull back the paper and cut along the outline of the molding.

7 Brush the paper into place using the bristles to push it into the edge.

77 PAPERING BEHIND RADIATORS

In most cases, it is easier to hang wallpaper behind a wall-mounted radiator, following one of the two methods below, than to remove the radiator. You can hang the wallpaper in either one or two lengths.

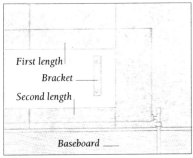

TWO LENGTHS
Hang a length from the ceiling to the bracket securing the radiator, and another from the bracket to the baseboard.

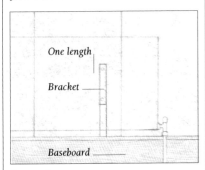

SINGLE LENGTH
Measure from the baseboard to the top of the bracket. Cut out a section of the paper for the bracket and pull the paper over it.

78 THE FINISHING TOUCH

Decorative borders add a final touch to a wallpapered room; hang at different heights for varied effects.

1 Use a level to mark the line where you intend to hang the border. Cut the border paper into lengths.

2 Apply wallpaper paste to the border paper and fold accordian-style, as you would with wallpaper (*see p.45.*)

3 Hang the top edge of the border paper and unfold the accordian fold by fold. Smooth with a paper brush as you go.

79 SOLVING WALLPAPER PROBLEMS

The majority of faults that occur on a wallpapered surface are caused by inadequate preparation of the surface, or insufficient paste or size, or the use of an incompatible paste or size. Vinyl paper, which is bought prepasted, is easy to hang, and the inexperienced decorator may find it simpler to handle. Most faults can be remedied without stripping off the paper. However, damp patches and brown spots (which may indicate a fungus) may require the wallpaper to be stripped.

BUBBLES
Pierce with a craft knife. Apply paste behind the opening. Smooth with a brush and wipe off any excess paste.

LOOSE SEAMS
Lift the loose seam with a knife and apply paste with a small brush. Smooth down the seam with a seam roller.

SHINY PATCHES
If shiny patches appear on the surface of matte paper, rub them with a ball of soft white bread.

CREASES
Cut the crease with a sharp craft knife or razor blade, apply more paste, and smooth into place with a roller.

MISMATCH
Pattern mismatches are difficult to avoid. However, they can be hidden if you finish in an unobtrusive place.

FLATTENED RELIEF
Do not use a seam roller with relief paper. Use a damp cloth to press down the edges: this will prevent flattening.

DAMP PATCHES
Not usually due to a wallpapering fault, damp patches may indicate a problem with the wall. Seek expert advice.

BROWN SPOTS
Brown spots usually indicate a fault in the wall. Strip the paper, treat the damp, and apply fungicidal paste.

PREPARING TO TILE

80 WHAT YOU NEED

Although most tiling equipment is inexpensive, some tools, in particular those used for cutting, can be costly. Many tile dealers will lend you tools.

ADHESIVE

HALF-MATCHSTICKS

NOTCHED SPREADER   PLASTIC SPACERS   POINTING TROWEL

△ TILING TOOLS
These tools are required to lay and spread adhesive, and to space the tiles.

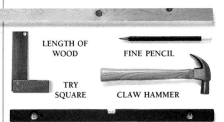

LENGTH OF WOOD   FINE PENCIL

TRY SQUARE   CLAW HAMMER

LARGE LEVEL

△ MEASURING & ALIGNING
Position the tiles with a batten and align them correctly with a level and try square.

SILICONE CAULK & GUN

DOWEL

SPONGE

TILE SAW

TILE CUTTER

SCORE-AND-SNAP PLIERS

TILE FILE

NIPPERS

READY-MIXED GROUT

POWER DRILL

△ CUTTING TOOLS
Use score-and-snap pliers to cut tiles, a file to smooth edges, and nippers to nibble edges.

△ FINISHING OFF
Buy grout to fill gaps between tiles and silicone to seal joins between surfaces.

81 HOW TO ESTIMATE QUANTITIES

Measure the length and width of the surface area to be tiled and multiply one measurement by the other. To determine the number of tiles required for a given area, consult the chart below (the number will depend on the size of tile). If you are not using square tiles, make a tiling gauge (see p.61) to help calculate how many tiles you need.

Size of tile	Area to be tiled in Square Feet (equivalent to 30 sq cm)					
	1	2	3	4	5	6
1 x 1 in (2.5 x 2.5 cm)	144	288	432	576	720	864
2 x 2 in (5 x 5 cm)	36	72	108	144	180	216
3 x 3 in (7 x 7 cm)	16	32	48	64	80	96
4 x 4 in (10 x 10 cm)	9	18	27	36	45	54
6 x 6 in (15 x 15 cm)	4	8	12	16	20	24
12 x 12 in (30 x 30 cm)	1	2	3	4	5	6

82 PREPARING WALL SURFACES

Good surface preparation is very important – tiles will reveal any flaws in the wall. The surface must be even and dry. Fill any holes (see p.11) and if a surface is very poor, replaster. It is essential that the surface be dry: damp patches will make tiles slip off eventually. Make sure you choose a suitable grouting and adhesive for the tile.

OLD PAINT
Roughen a painted surface with coarse sandpaper. Strip off any flaking paint with a scraper.

OLD WALLPAPER
Strip off the old wallpaper and lining paper. Fill any holes and make the surface as smooth as possible.

OLD TILES
Remove old tiles with a wide chisel and sledge hammer (wear goggles). Replaster the surface.

83 FIND A LEVEL STARTING POINT

One of the most important preparatory steps to good tiling is to ensure the correct alignment of the tiles. Never assume that the edges of windows, floors, or baseboards are true. A level or plumb line will help you lay the tiles in true horizontal and vertical rows. Always begin tiling at the bottom of the wall and work your way upward.

1 Place the tile against the top edge of the baseboard. Nail a batten above the tile with just one nail, leaving a small gap for grouting between the tile and batten. Pivot to find the horizontal.

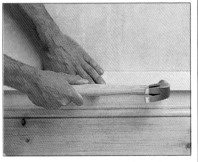

2 Hold a level against the batten to check that its horizontal alignment is correct. Lightly nail the batten in place at intervals along its length. If tiling over old tiles, screw the batten in place.

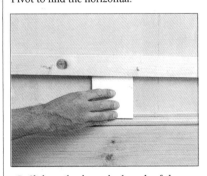

3 Slide a tile along the length of the batten between it and the top of the baseboard. Mark the upper edge of the tile on the wall at the shortest point. Remove the batten.

4 Draw a horizontal line where the mark lies. Nail the batten to the wall so that its upper edge is aligned with the line. Begin tiling above this line. You may have to cut tiles to fill the gap below.

84 HOW TO MAKE A TILING GAUGE

You use a tiling gauge to calculate the number of tiles needed for the vertical length. To make the gauge, lay a length of batten against a row of tiles, leaving space to allow for grouting. Mark the tile widths. When you have established a starting point (*see step 3, p.60*), place the gauge on the mark and work up the wall.

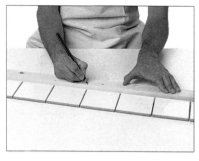

MARK TILE WIDTHS ON THE BATTEN

85 PREPARING TO TILE

Lay a row of whole tiles on a horizontal surface directly below the area to be tiled. Allow spaces in between each tile. You may not be able to fill the area with whole tiles. Aim, however, to center the whole tiles, leaving room for a "border" of cut tiles all around (*see p.63*).

1 Mark the edge of the first tile on the top surface of the batten. The tiling will begin at this point. Establish a true vertical to the mark with a chalk line. If a wall is to be only partly tiled, mark on the wall where the tiling stops.

2 Hold another batten against the wall so that its inner edge is aligned with the vertical line on the wall and the mark on the horizontal batten. Then attach the batten to the wall with nails lightly hammered in at 4 in (10 cm) intervals.

HANGING WALL TILES

86 APPLYING WHOLE TILES

When both the battens are in place (see pp.60–61), you can begin tiling. Only remove the battens when you have finished tiling the central area and are ready to tile the perimeter, for which you may need cut tiles. Set aside damaged tiles to use as cut tiles. Before you start to tile, check the corner made by the two battens to ensure that the battens are securely attached. Place a try square into the corner. If the corner is not square, adjust the battens. Consult the manufacturer's instructions for the correct adhesive. Use plastic spacers or matchsticks to space the tiles.

1 Use a pointing trowel to apply adhesive in 1 sq yd (1 sq m) sections.

2 Spread the adhesive evenly with a notched spreader held at a 45° angle to the wall. The ridges create suction.

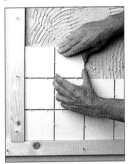

3 Start tiling in the corner, working along the horizontal line. Place spacers after each tile to position them evenly.

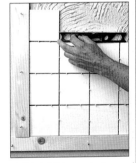

4 Wait 12 hours before removing the battens. Grout over the spacers (if you have used matchsticks as spacers, remove them).

87 HOW TO SCORE TILES

You need to score a tile before cutting it. Begin by drawing a line along the edge of the tile with a soft pencil. Hold a try square along the pencil mark, and carefully score through the tile's glaze with the tip of a scorer in one firm stroke. Alternatively, you can use the wheel cutter of score-and-snap pliers to score a tile; again, use the edge of the try square as a guide.

TILE SCORER

88 CUTTING TILES

Once you have scored the tile, break it over two matchsticks, or use score-and-snap pliers. Both methods give the tile a clean edge.

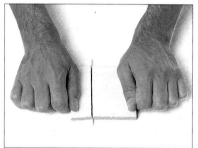

△ USING MATCHSTICKS
Place two matchsticks on a firm surface and the tile on top. Press down firmly.

◁ USING SCORE-AND-SNAP PLIERS
Put the line on the tile in the center of the pinching plate. Squeeze the handles together.

89 TRIMMING TILES

Use a tile nipper to neaten the edges of cut tiles, or to trim, instead of cutting a small area off a tile. Start by scoring the tile, making sure that you penetrate the glaze. Then use the nipper to snip bits of tile away up to the marked line. Once you have nipped the tile, file it to make a clean edge: rub the cut edge over the file, occasionally shaking the dust from the file mesh.

TILE NIPPER

90 CUTTING CURVES

It is sometimes necessary to cut a curve in a tile to fit it around a fixture such as a pipe or a basin. A tile saw and a vise are essential for good results. After cutting a tile, use a file to smooth its edges.

1 Cut a piece of paper to the tile shape and fit it against the curve – a series of cuts will help it fit. Mark the curve on the paper.

2 Cut along the curved line. Place the paper template on the tile. Draw around the curve using a china marker.

3 Score along the line. Place the tile in a vise and cut out the scored curve with a tile saw. Apply gentle pressure.

91 TILING INTERNAL CORNERS

Lay whole tiles along the front edge and cut tiles along the back of a recess. When you apply adhesive to cut tiles, it is easier to spread it onto the surface that you are tiling, rather than the tile itself.

1 Lay a tile against the back wall and mark where it overlaps the last row of whole tiles. Allow for grouting, and cut to fit.

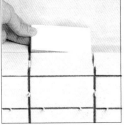

2 Smooth the tile edges by filing. Position the tile so that the cut edge lies in the corner to give a neat appearance.

EXTERNAL CORNERS
Lay on least visible side of corner first, with glazed edges on most visible side.

92 GROUTING TILES

When the tile adhesive is dry (it takes approximately 12 hours), fill the spaces between the tiles with grout. Several different types of grout are available; some are water-resistant; others are completely waterproof. Check the instructions to make sure that you are buying the right type for your particular use. If you buy powdered grout, you will have to mix it with water; alternatively, buy it premixed in tubs. Work over areas of 1 sq yd (1 sq m) at a time and always wipe away excess grout before it dries.

1 Using a squeegee, apply the grout to the gaps between the tiles.

2 Work the grout into the joints. Wipe away any excess with a sponge.

3 As the grout hardens, draw a piece of dowel along the joints.

4 Wipe off excess grout and polish the surface with a soft, dry cloth.

93 HOW TO APPLY TILE SEALANT

When the grout is dry (check the package for the drying time), apply silicone sealant to where the tiled area meets another surface. Apply the sealant from the tube or trigger-action cartridge. Make sure it fills the gap. Draw a wet finger across the sealant to smooth it, and wipe away any excess with a damp cloth.

FILL THE GAP BETWEEN TILES AND BATH

94 Applying Fixtures

An electric drill and masonry drill bit are essential if you want to attach a fixture to a tiled surface, as you will need to drill a hole for the screw. You will also need a strip of masking tape, a pencil, a scorer, and, ideally, someone to hold a vacuum cleaner nozzle under the hole as you drill. Push the wallplugs right into the wall and not just into the tiles: if they are not fixed securely into the wall, they will fall out.

1 Hold the fixture against the tiles. Mark the top drilling point with a soft pencil or china marker. (If you put in one screw and hang the fixture, you can position the other holes.)

2 Make the initial hole with a sharp tool such as the tip of a tile scorer. Press the tip of the scorer firmly onto the pencil mark and rotate the scorer to make a hole.

3 Put down a piece of masking tape across the hole to help steady the drill. Mark the tape, and drill into the tile at a slow speed. Press lightly and drill into the wall itself.

95 Cleaning Tiles

Wipe tiles over with a damp cloth to clean. Keeping grout clean can be more difficult. It can become discolored quickly, especially if it is in a kitchen or bathroom area. Occasionally, grout in a very moist area can mildew or grow mold. Grout will last longer if you use the appropriate type; for example, use waterproof grout for showers.

- Remove dirt from grouting with an old toothbrush and a solution of warm water and detergent.
- Improve the look of dirty grouting with a layer of whitener.
- If the grout is badly damaged, scrape it out and replace.
- Apply fungicide and then whitener to moldy grout or scrape out the grout and replace with new.

CLEANING UP

96 HOW TO CLEAN OFF LATEX PAINT

Follow the manufacturer's instructions to clean paintbrushes correctly. Generally, latex paint is easy to wash off. Scrape off the bulk of the paint from the brush with the blunt edge of a flat-bladed knife. Then run warm water over the brush as you gently splay out the bristles. Pay particular attention to the heel of the brush. Finish off by adding detergent, rinsing the brush, and giving it a good shake.

SPLAY THE BRISTLES UNDER WARM WATER

97 HOW TO CLEAN OFF OIL-BASED PAINT

As oil-based paint is not water soluble, it is more difficult to remove from equipment. Use mineral spirits or turpentine. Take safety precautions when using these solvents *(see p.19.)*

1 Squeeze and scrape the paint off the brush onto some newspaper. Dip the brush in a jar of solvent and stir.

2 Wash the brush with detergent and warm water, rinse, and shake dry. Remove all trace of the solvent.

98 PAINTBRUSH CARE

Protect paintbrushes when they are not in use but the project is still in progress. For temporary storage suspend a brush in a jar of water by drilling a hole through the brush handle and passing a wire through it, or wrap the brush in aluminum foil. Once cleaned and dried, store brushes on their sides with an elastic band stretched around the bristles. Wrap them in paper or lint-free cloth.

SUSPENDED BRUSH

WRAPPED IN FOIL

WRAPPED IN ELASTIC BAND

WRAPPED IN PAPER

99 HOW TO CLEAN ROLLERS & PADS

Ideally, clean paint pads and rollers immediately after use. As they are usually used with latex paint, they are easy to clean. If they are to last, pads and rollers should be stored in a dry, well-ventilated area, wrapped in paper or lint-free cloth. Do not use solvents such as turpentine on pads as they may damage the pad. Clean off paint with lukewarm water and detergent. Solvents can be used on rollers.

△ REMOVING PAINT
To clean off paint from a roller or pad, roll it over several layers of newspaper. Keep putting new layers of newspaper down so that the roller does not reabsorb paint.

△ FINAL RINSE
Remove the sleeve from the roller cage and, if necessary, clean with a solvent. Wash the roller, or sleeve, or pad in warm water and detergent. Rinse and shake dry.

100 HOW TO WASH AWAY PASTE

Always clean wallpapering tools before storing them. Any tools that come into contact with wallpaper paste should be wiped as they are being used. Wipe down seam rollers, scissors, and pasting brushes with a damp, clean cloth. Wash the paste out of brushes with detergent and warm water. Shake out excess water and store in a dry place.

WASH WITH WARM WATER & DETERGENT

101 CLEANING TILING TOOLS

It is essential to clean tiling tools promptly after use, as tiling adhesive dries very quickly. Follow the adhesive manufacturer's instructions for cleaning. Most adhesives and sealants can be washed off in warm water without using a detergent. You should allow the tools to dry before you store them. Rinse off grout outdoors, or run plenty of water after cleaning to avoid clogging drains.

△ RINSE UNDER RUNNING WATER
Wash the pointing trowel and spreading tool in water. After drying the metal blade of the pointing trowel, coat it with oil to prevent rusting.

△ SOAK SPONGES THOROUGHLY
Rinse adhesive and grouting off the sponge with water. You will probably have to soak it several times to remove every last trace. Allow the sponge to dry before storing.

INDEX

ACKNOWLEDGMENTS

Dorling Kindersley would like to thank Julia Pashley for picture research, Hilary Bird for compiling the index, Ann Kay for proofreading, Cooling Brown for editorial assistance, Murdo Culver for design assistance, and Mark Bracey for computer assistance.

Photography
KEY: t *top*; b *bottom*; c *center*; l *left*; r *right*
All photographs by Tim Ridley except for:

Robert Harding Syndication/IPC Magazines Ltd.
Nick Carter 35br; J. Merrell 33tr; Trevor Richards 36br;
Peter Woloszynski 2 & 30cr; 28b.

Colin Walton: 3.

Illustrations
Andrew MacDonald